SOOKIE AND IVY

Sookie and Ivy

FRIENDS FOREVER!

JANI OJA

Don't miss our other book,
Every Day Is a Celebration!

© 2024 by Jani Oja and Fox Chapel Publishing Company, Inc.

Sookie and Ivy Friends Forever! is an original work, first published in 2024 by Fox Chapel Publishing Company, Inc.

All rights reserved. No part of this publication may be reproduced, stored in a retrieval system or transmitted, in any form or by any means, electronic, mechanical, photocopying, recording or otherwise, without the prior written permission of the copyright holders.

ISBN 978-1-4971-0526-3

The Cataloging-in-Publication Data is on file with the Library of Congress.

To learn more about the other great books from Fox Chapel Publishing, or to find a retailer near you, call toll-free

800-457-9112

or send mail to

903 Square Street

Mount Joy, PA 17552

or visit us at www.FoxChapelPublishing.com.

We are always looking for talented authors. To submit an idea, please send a brief inquiry to

acquisitions@foxchapelpublishing.com.

Printed in China

First printing

Sookie   Ivy

Hi There

Allow us to introduce ourselves. We're Sookie and Ivy, senior hat models and pawfessional food critics with a knack for making people smile. We were rescued as small girls, and now we spend our days in luxury, wearing silly hats that are designed and handmade by our mom. We're the ultimate besties, and we've shared every adventure for over a decade. Try not to be jealous, and don't let our serious faces fool you—we love the attention and are ready to "sit, stay, and cro-slay" as soon as our mom grabs her camera (and the treatos!). This book is a celebration of our timeless friendship, and the beauty of friendship all around the world!

"To the world you may be just one person, but to one person you may be the world."

–Dr. Seuss

"Every night is girls night."

–BARBIE, *BARBIE*

"I have so mushroom in my heart for you."

–SOOKIE AND IVY

"Friendship is born at that moment
when one person says to another,
'What! You too? I thought I was the only one.'"

–C.S. LEWIS

SOOKIEANDIVY

"A true friend is someone who thinks that you are a good egg even though he knows that you are slightly cracked."

–BERNARD MELTZER

"Things are never quite as scary
when you've got a best friend."

–BILL WATTERSON

"A friend knows the song in my heart and sings it to me when my memory fails."

–DONNA ROBERTS

"She's my friend because we both know what it's like to have people be jealous of us."

−CHER, *CLUELESS*

SOOKIEANDIVY

"A good friend is like a four-leaf clover;
hard to find and lucky to have."

–IRISH PROVERB

"I couldn't ask for a batter friend."

–Sookie and Ivy

"If you are ever lucky enough to find a weirdo,
never let them go."

–Matthew Gray Gubler

"Some people are worth melting for."

–OLAF, *FROZEN*

SOOKIEANDIVY

"If there ever comes a day when
we can't be together, keep me in your heart.
I'll stay there forever."

–Winnie the Pooh

SOOKIEANDIVY

"Keep the ones who heard you
when you never said a word."

–JON YORK

"True friends stick by you, no matter what."

–RUDOLPH, *RUDOLPH THE RED-NOSED REINDEER*

"Friends are the sprinkles
on the donuts of life."

–SOOKIE AND IVY

"Friendship can be so comfortable,
but nurture it—don't take it for granted."

–BETTY WHITE

"I will not let you go into the unknown alone."

–BRAM STOKER

sniffspection

"A friend is one who overlooks your broken fence and admires the flowers in your garden."

–Unknown

"We didn't realize we were making memories,
we just knew we were having fun."

–A.A. MILNE

"Friendship isn't a big thing—
it's a million little things."

–Paulo Coelho

"One of the most beautiful qualities
of true friendship is to understand
and to be understood."

–LUCIUS ANNAEUS SENECA

"I cherry-ish our friendship."

–SOOKIE AND IVY

"When you can't look on the bright side,
I will sit with you in the dark."

–Lewis Carroll

"That's what friends do;
they forgive each other."

–DONKEY, *SHREK*

SOOKIEANDIVY

"We go together like burgers and fries."

–Sookie and Ivy

"The most beautiful discovery true friends make is that they can grow separately without growing apart."

–Elisabeth Foley

"A friend is someone to share the last cookie with."

–Cookie Monster, *Sesame Street*

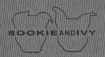

"You've bean my very best friend."

–Sookie and Ivy

Paint Night "Lick Art"

Materials: Canvas, acrylic paint, pressed flowers, freezer bag, peanut butter*

Instructions: On a blank canvas, add paint. Place the canvas in a freezer bag, and drizzle natural peanut butter on top of bag. Allow your dog to lick up the peanut butter, then carefully remove the canvas from the bag. Add pressed flowers before the paint dries.

Do not give dogs peanut butter with xylitol (aka birch sugar); it is extremely toxic.

SOOKIEANDIVY

About the Author and Doggos

Jani Oja was born in Finland and currently resides in Massachusetts with her husband and two rescue dogs, Sookie and Ivy. She is a self-taught crochet artist and hobby photographer, and shares Sookie and Ivy's adventures on social media to their two million supporters. Sookie and Ivy were both adopted from animal shelters in Florida, and Ivy, in particular, came from a rough beginning. The pair are lovingly known as "the gorls," and Jani hopes their silly videos and photo content can help teach people to not judge dogs based on their appearance. The gorls were destined to spread smiles, and are tail-wagging ready to create content as soon as Jani starts to set up their recording area. To see Sookie and Ivy's full hat collection spanning over 100 sets, connect with Jani on social media (@sookieandivy on all platforms).